MISSOURI'S WILD HORSES

AND THE LAND THEY ROAM

ALBERT ALLEN

iUniverse books may be ordered through booksellers or by contacting:

iUniverse
1663 Liberty Drive
Bloomington, IN 47403
www.iuniverse.com
844-349-9409

Because of the dynamic nature of the Internet, any web addresses or links contained in this book may have changed since publication and may no longer be valid. The views expressed in this work are solely those of the author and do not necessarily reflect the views of the publisher, and the publisher hereby disclaims any responsibility for them.

ISBN: 978-1-6632-5097-1 (sc)
ISBN: 978-1-6632-5098-8 (e)

Library of Congress Control Number: 2023903547

Print information available on the last page.

iUniverse rev. date: 03/07/2023

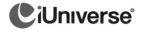

MISSOURI'S WILD HORSES AND
THE LAND THEY ROAM

Author and Photographer
Albert Allen

Other books by the author:
The Mooroos
Life's Lamplighters

MISSOURI'S WILD HORSES

Dedicated to all Carter and Shannon County residents and others who so diligently worked to protect the wild horses that now legally roam free along the banks of Big Shawnee Creek, Little Shawnee Creek, Rocky Creek, and Rogers Creek as well as the Current and Jacks Fork Rivers within the Ozark National Scenic Riverways

ALBERT L. ALLEN
AUTHOR &
PHOTOGRAPHER
Book II

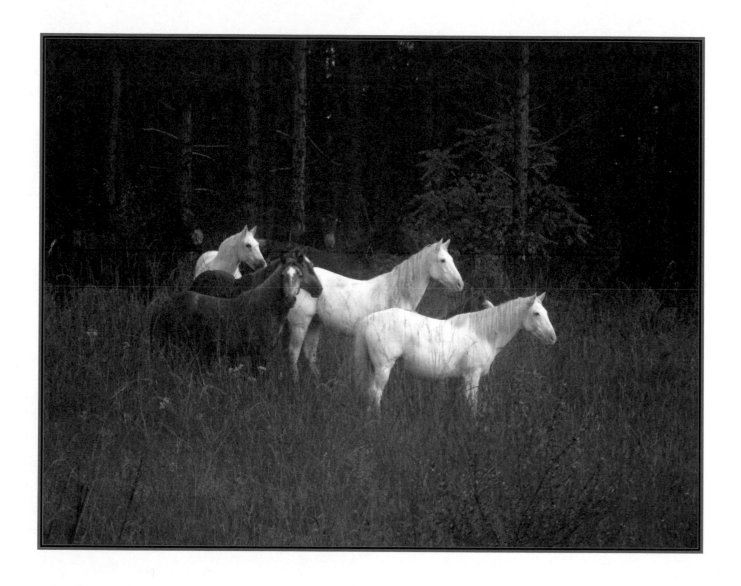

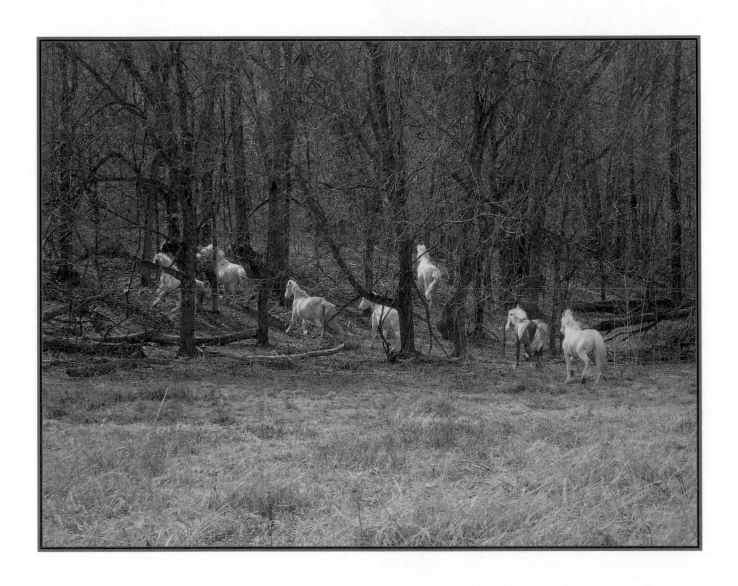

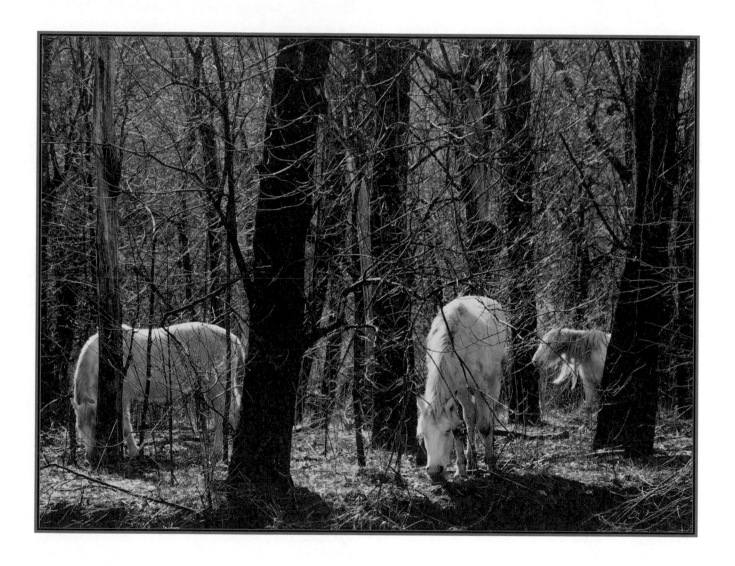

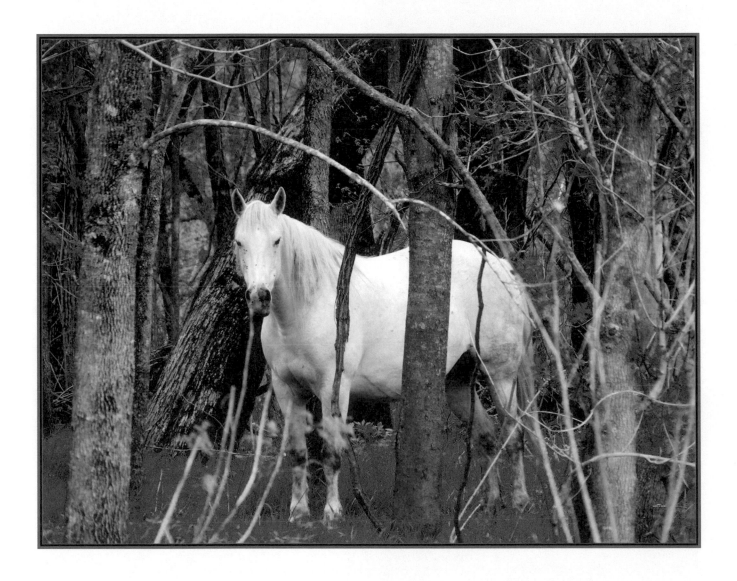

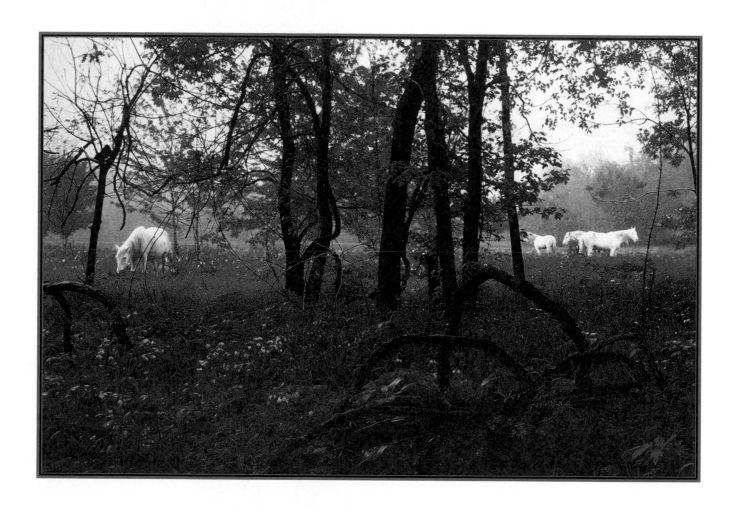

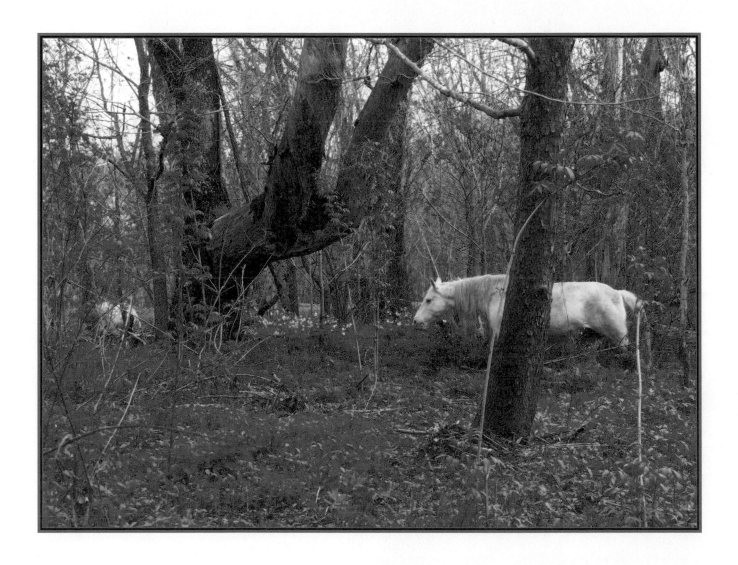

ALBERT ALLEN

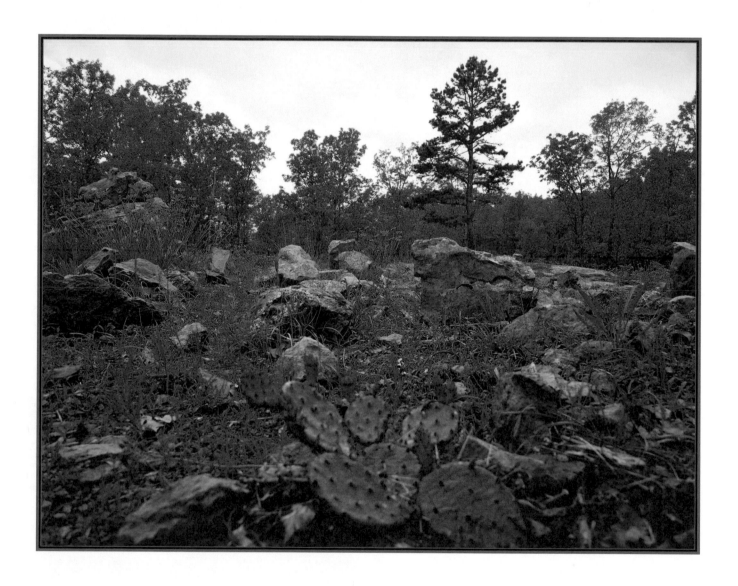

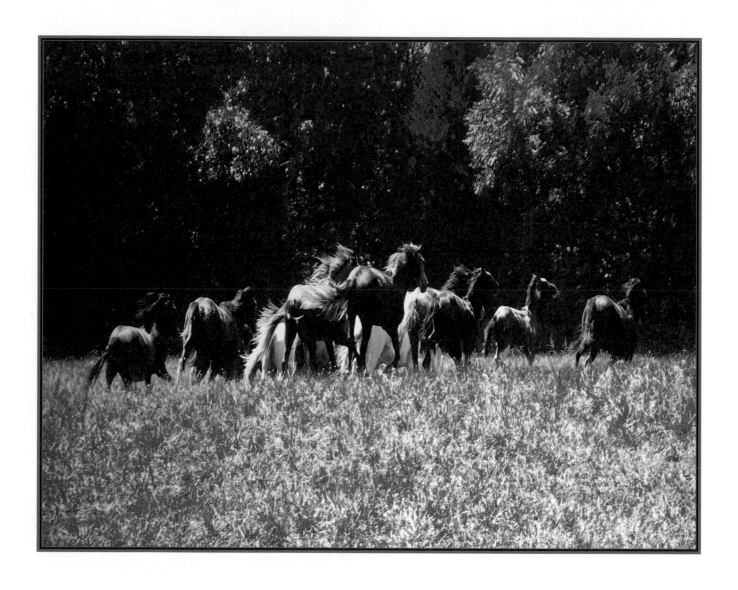

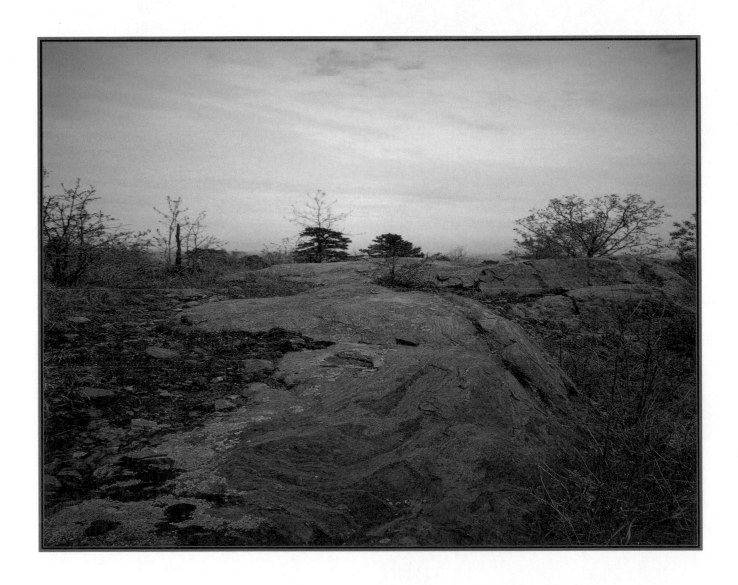

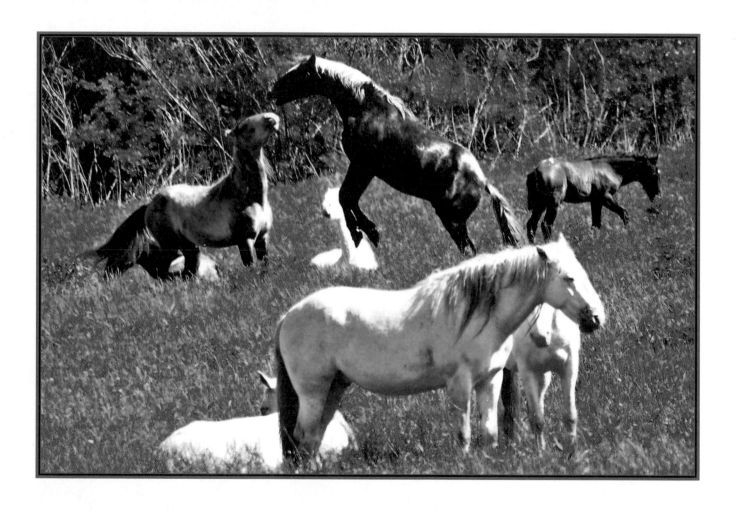

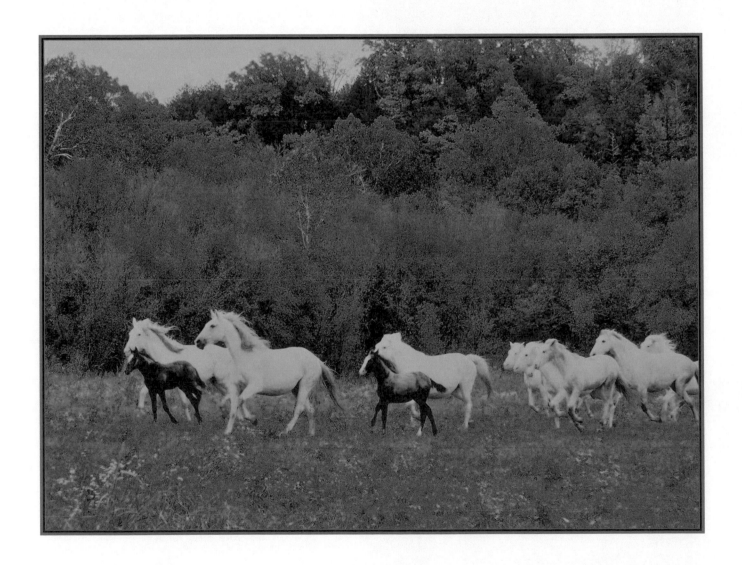

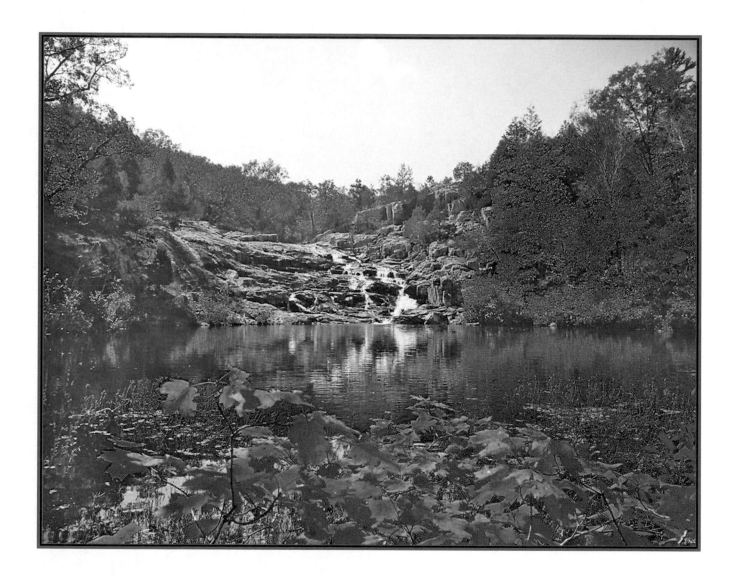

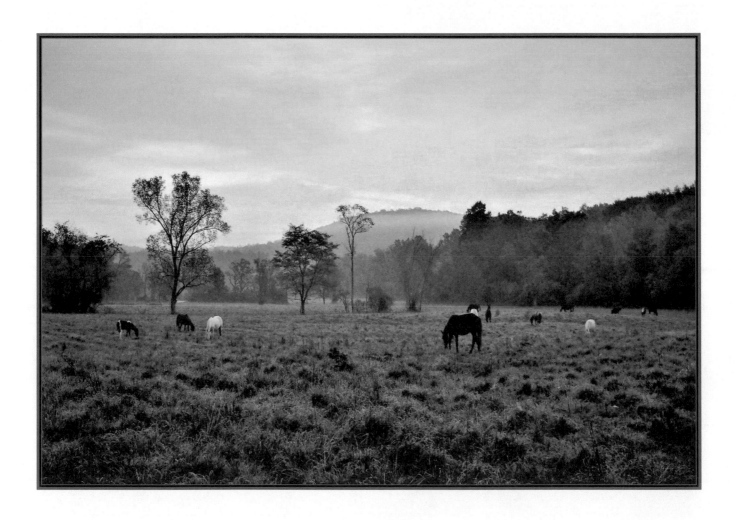

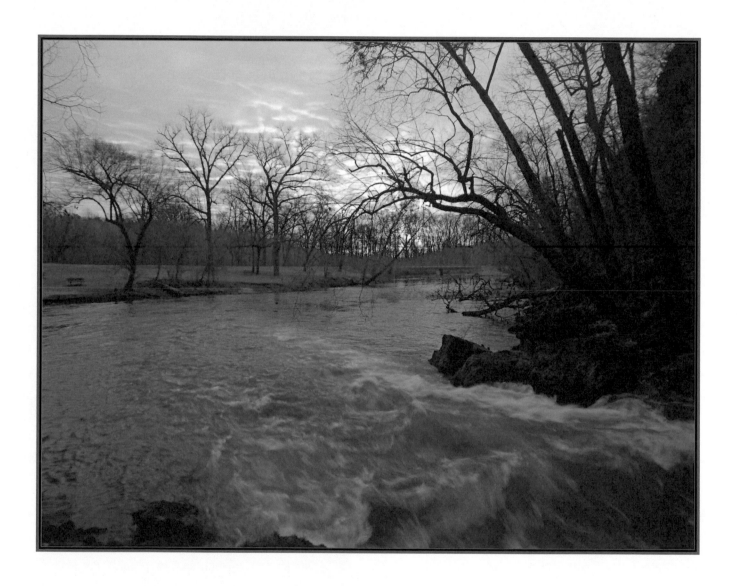

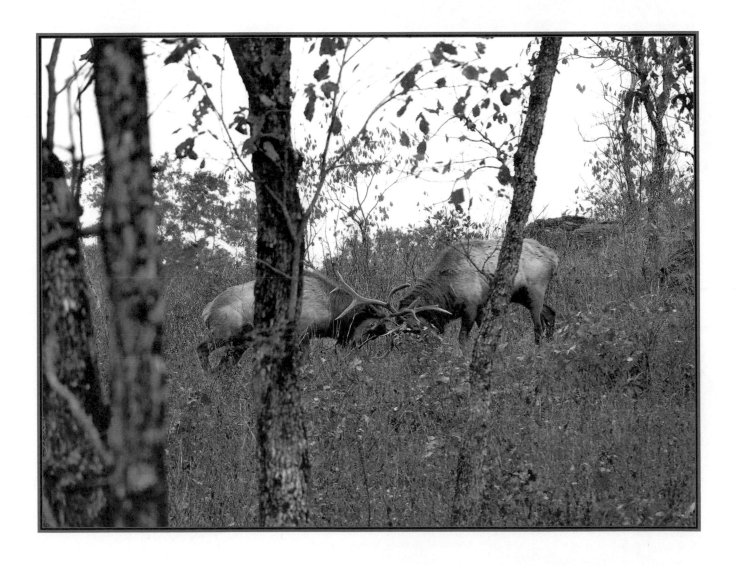

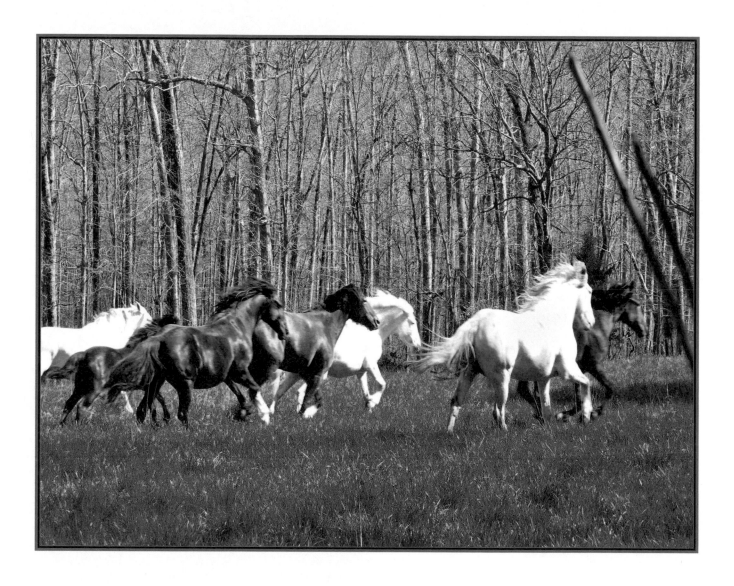

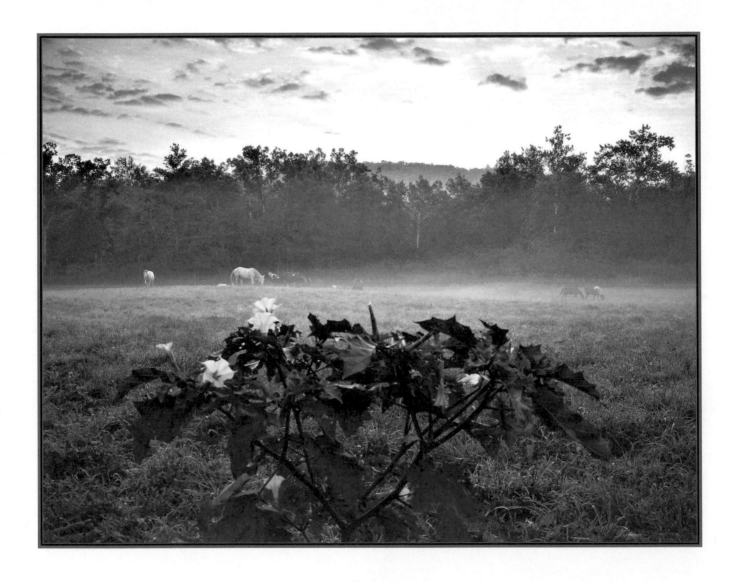

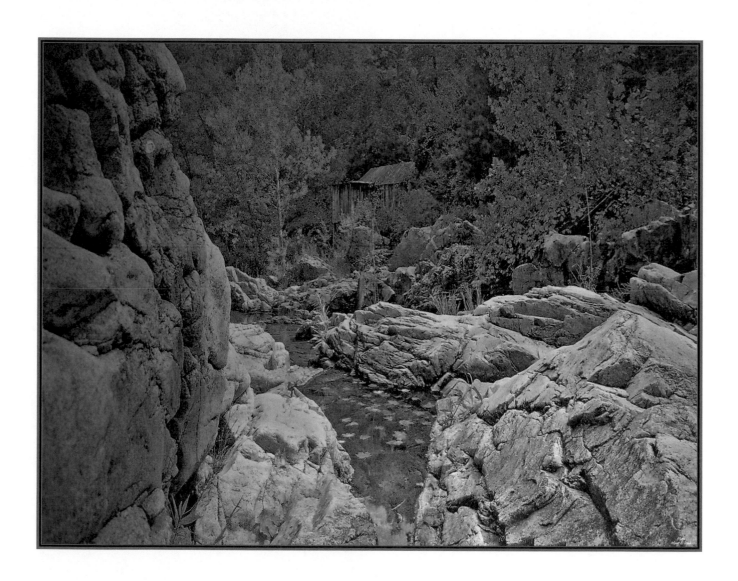

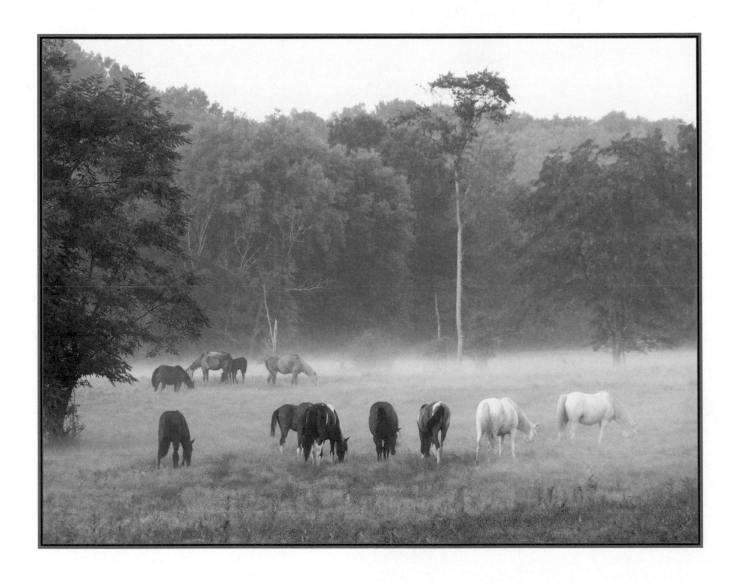

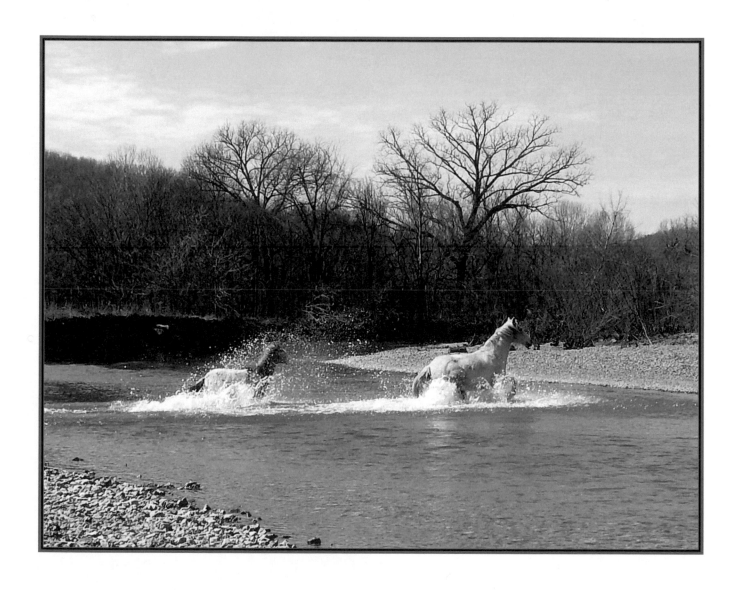

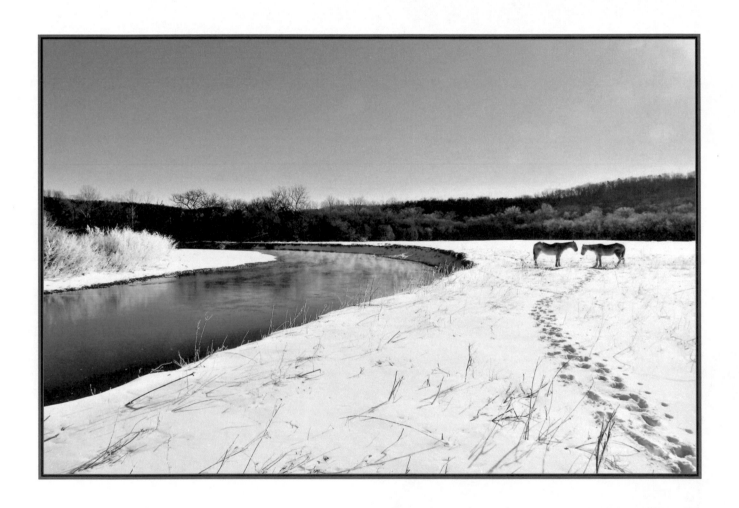

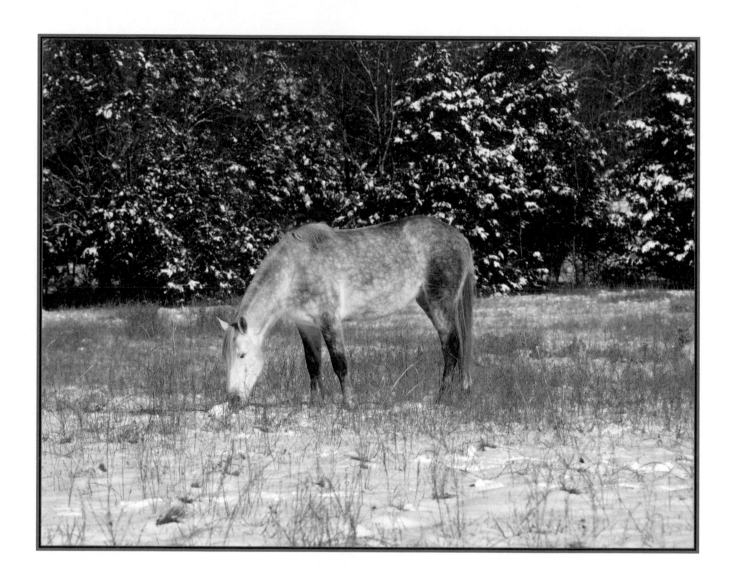

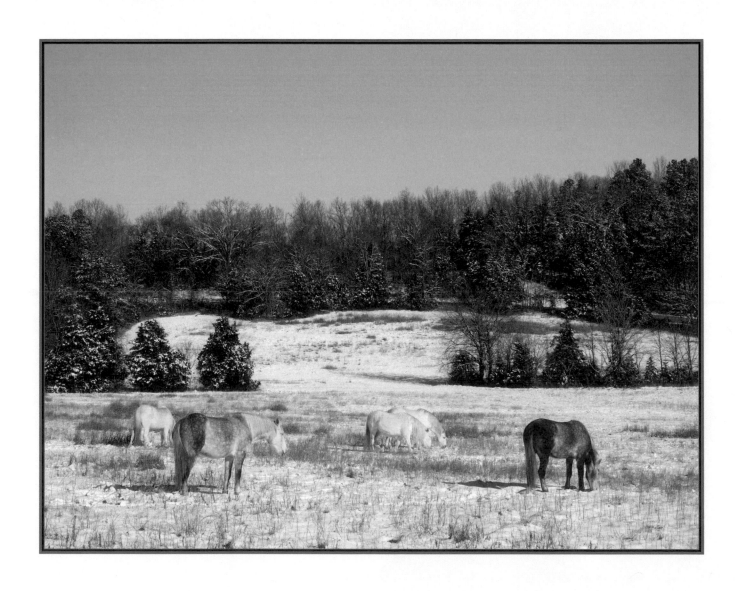

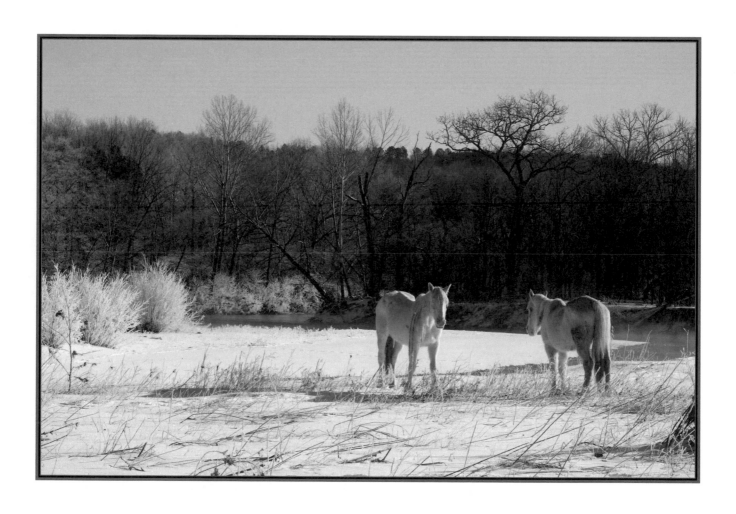

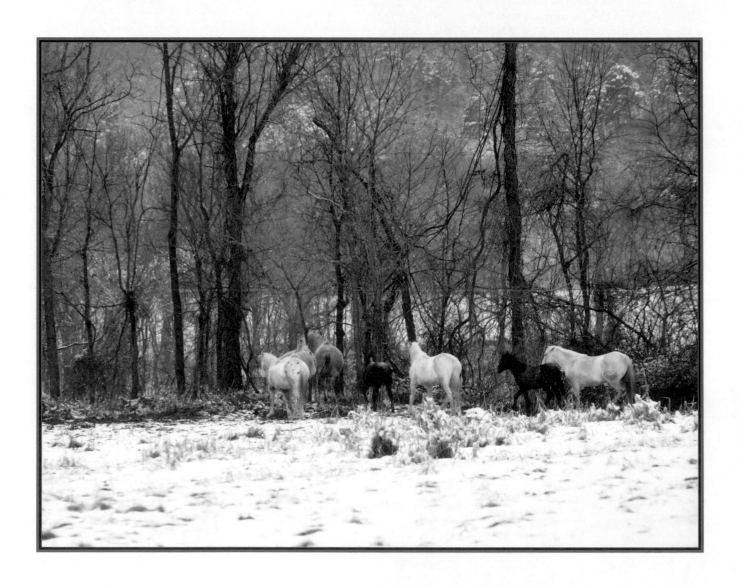

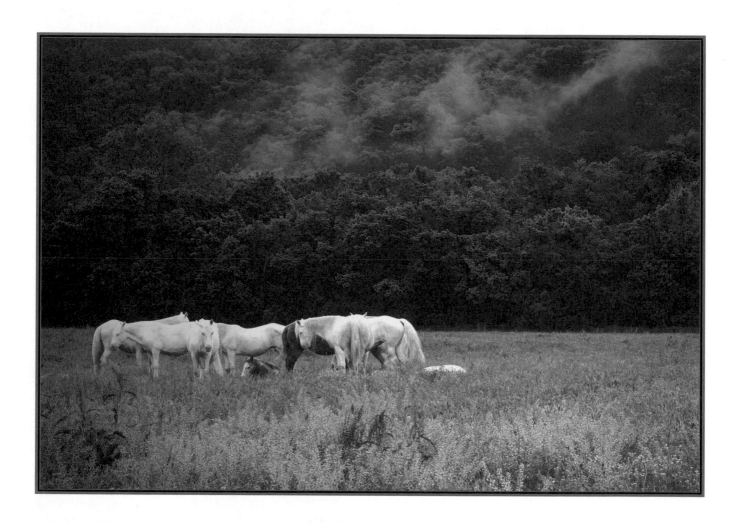

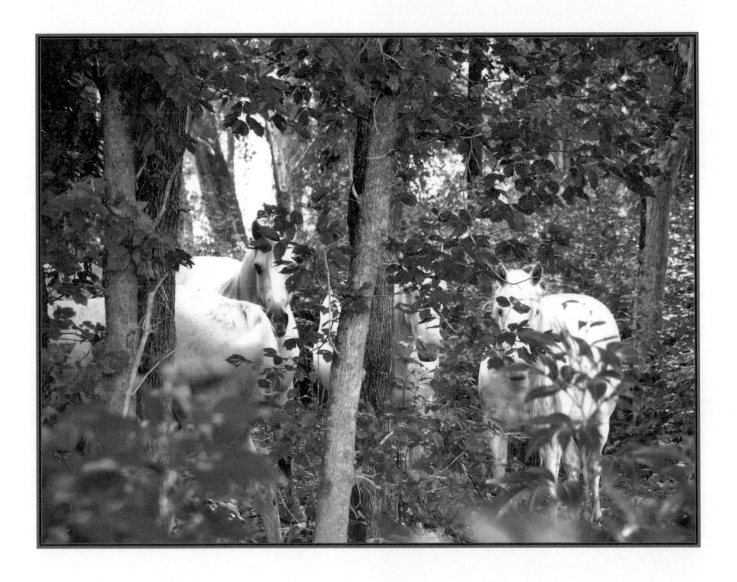

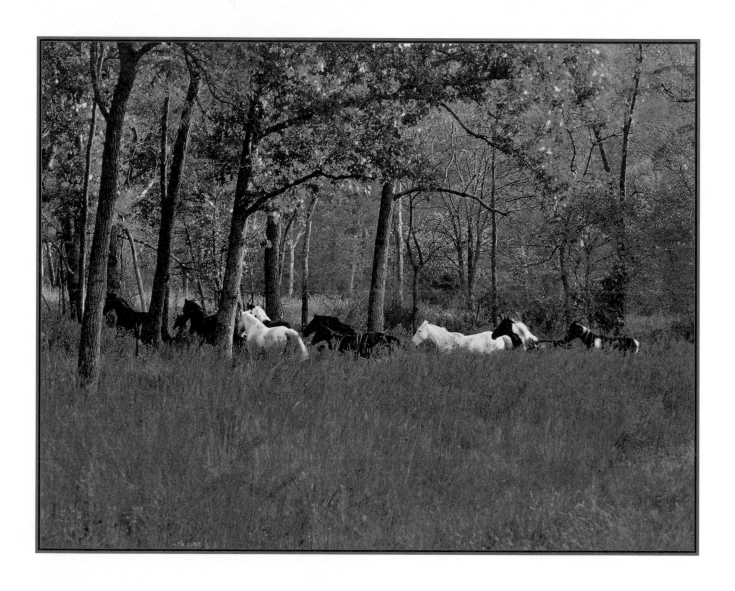

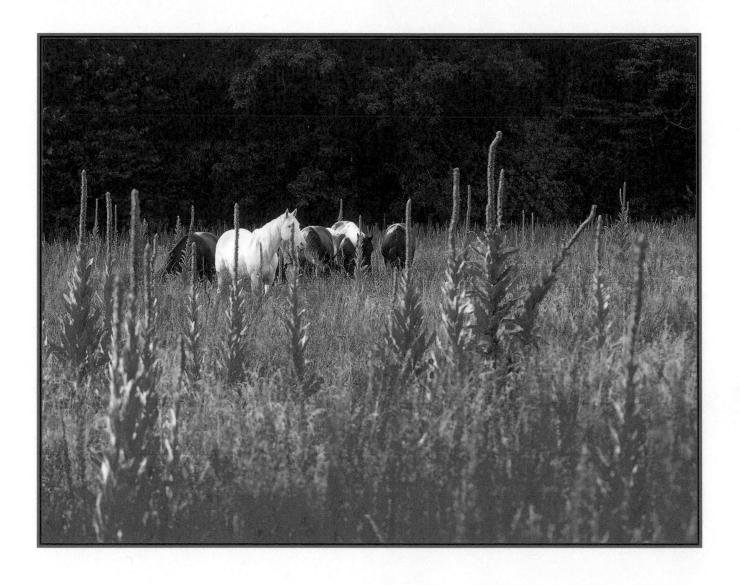

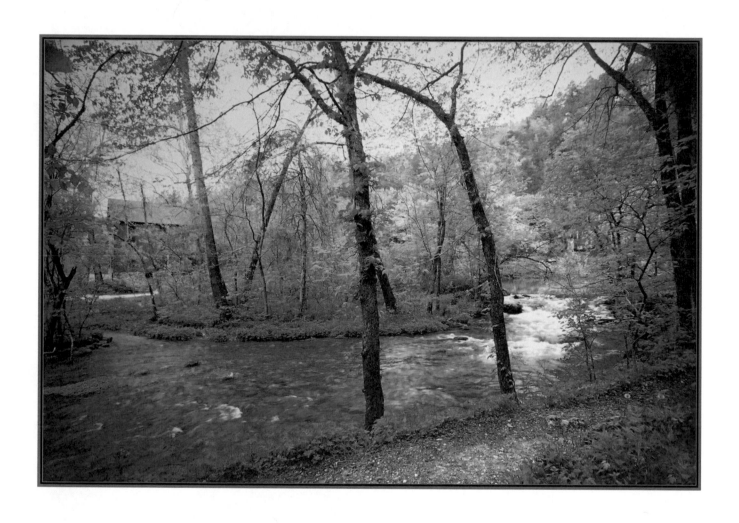

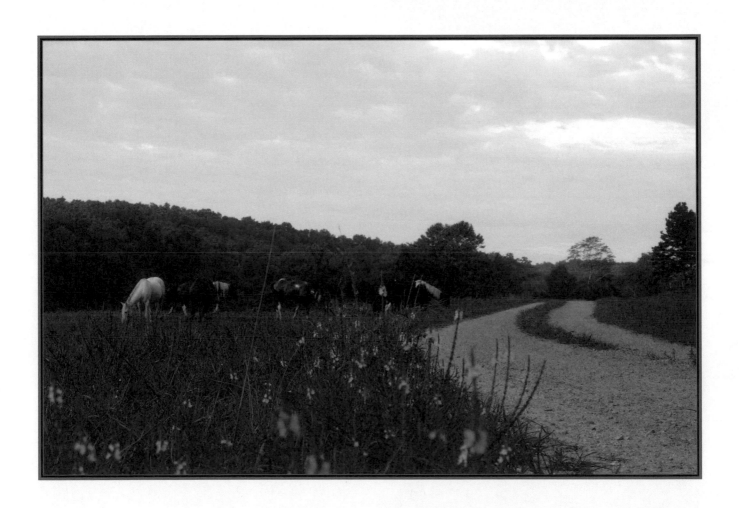

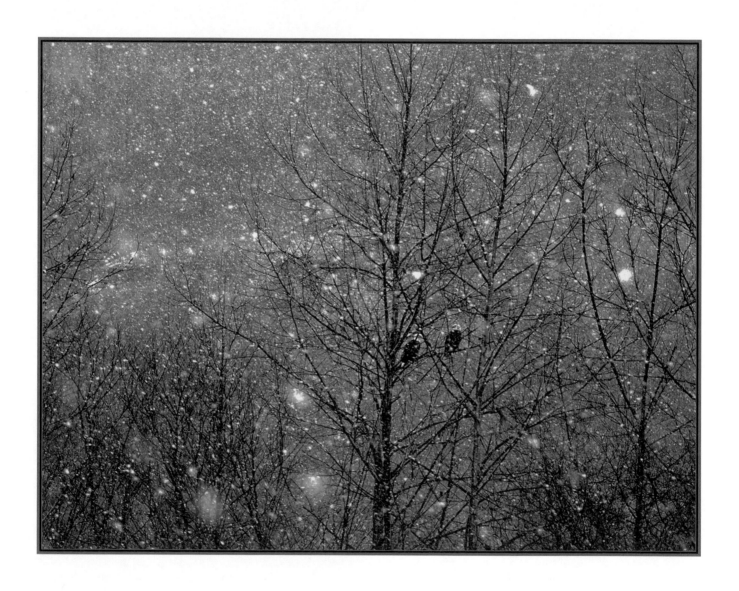

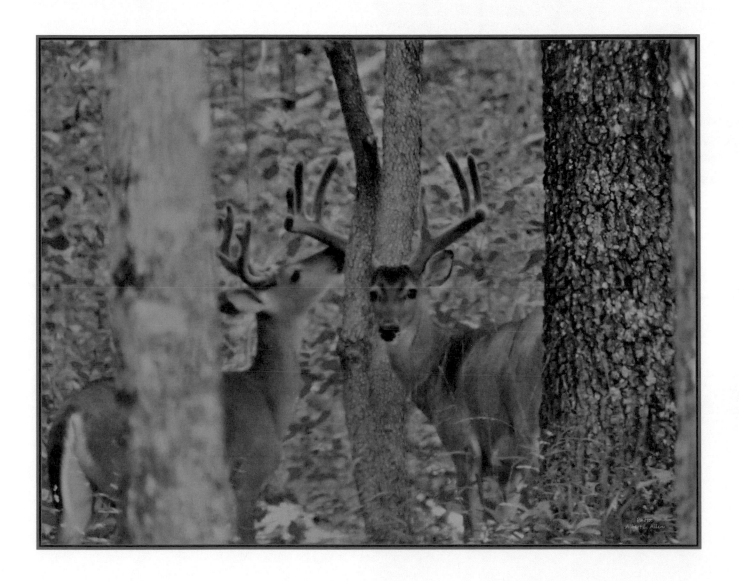

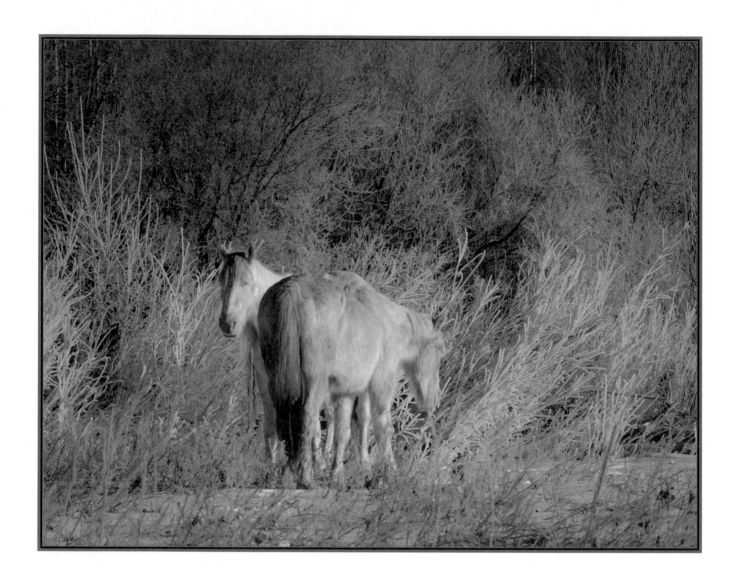

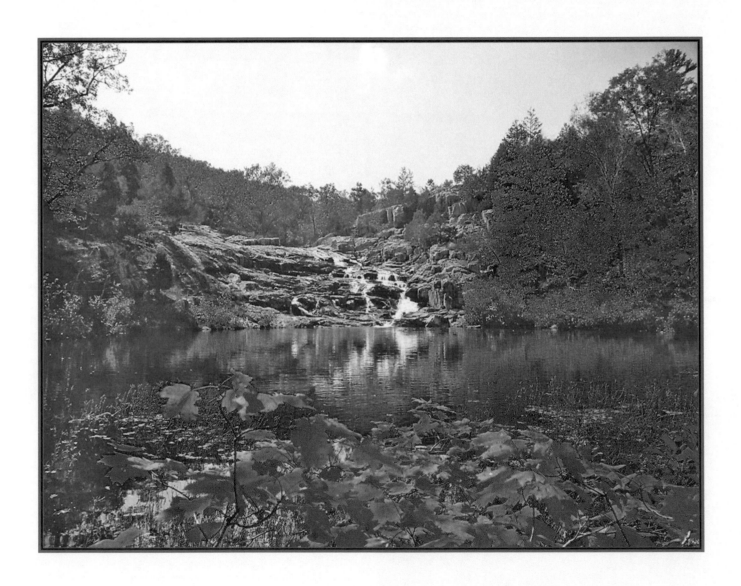

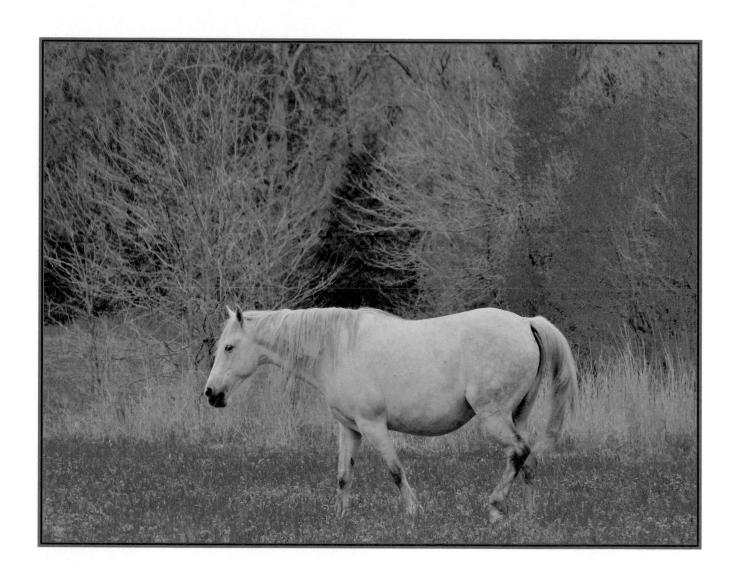

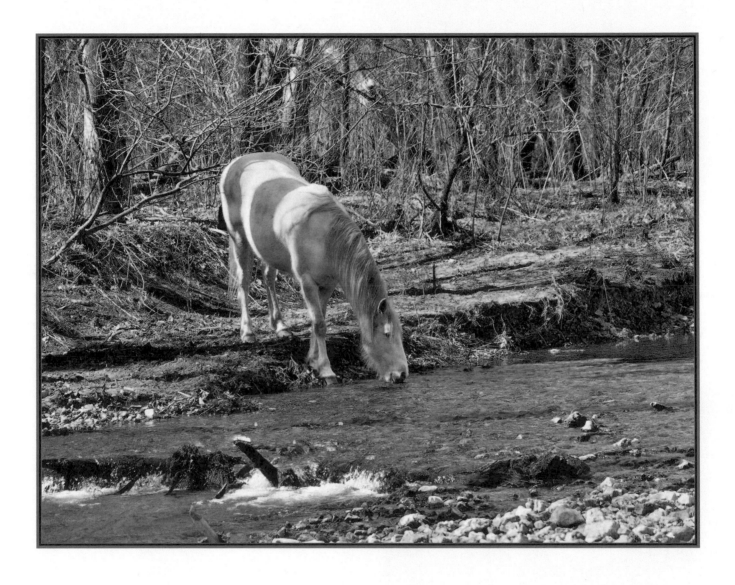

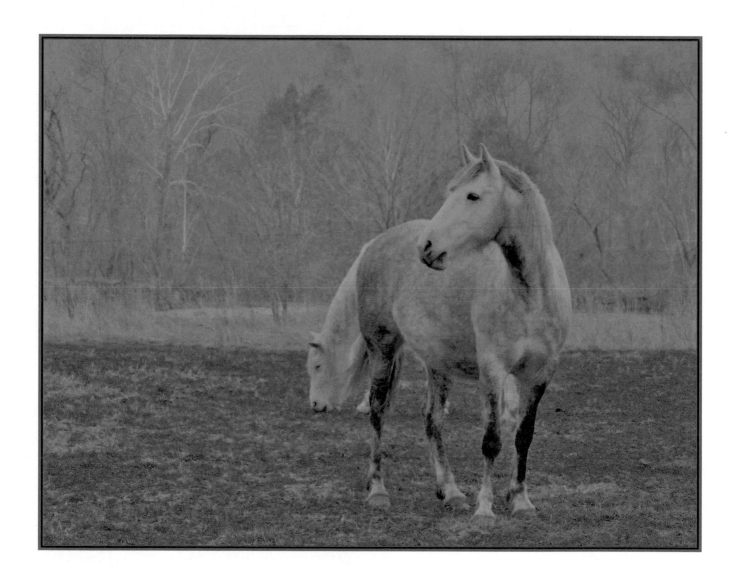

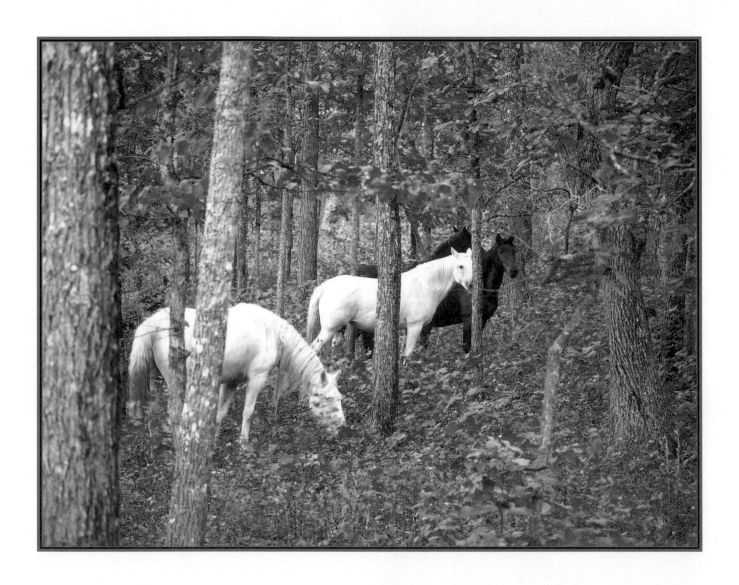

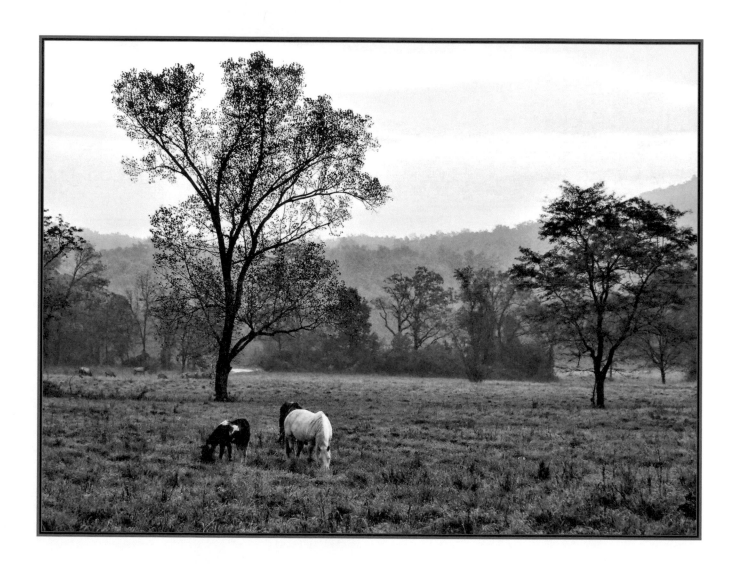

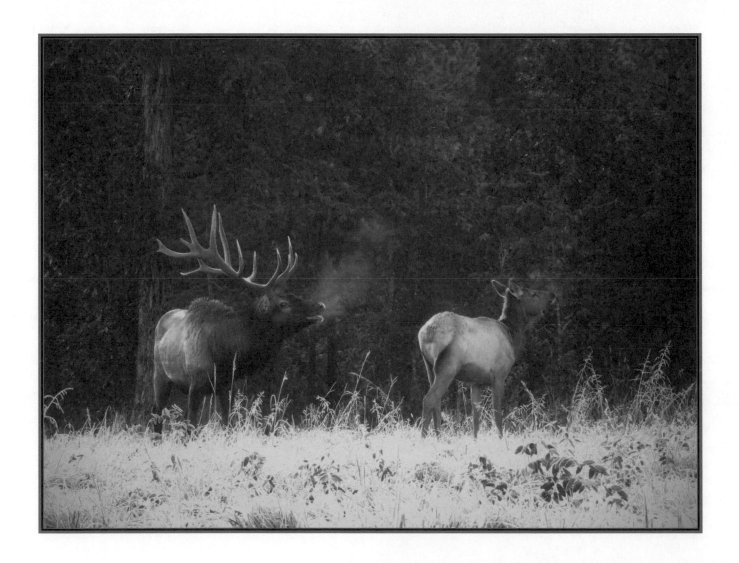

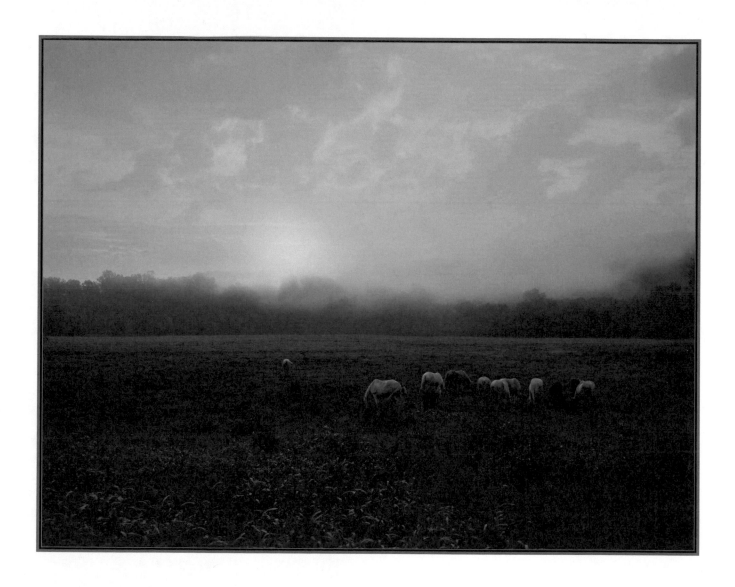

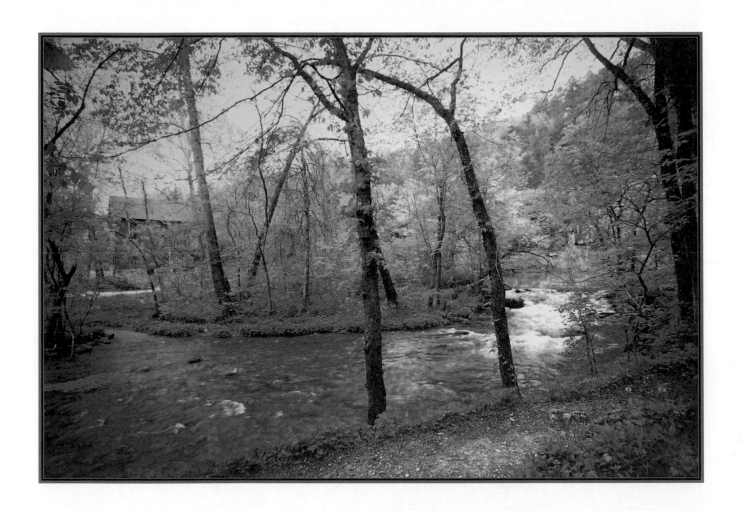

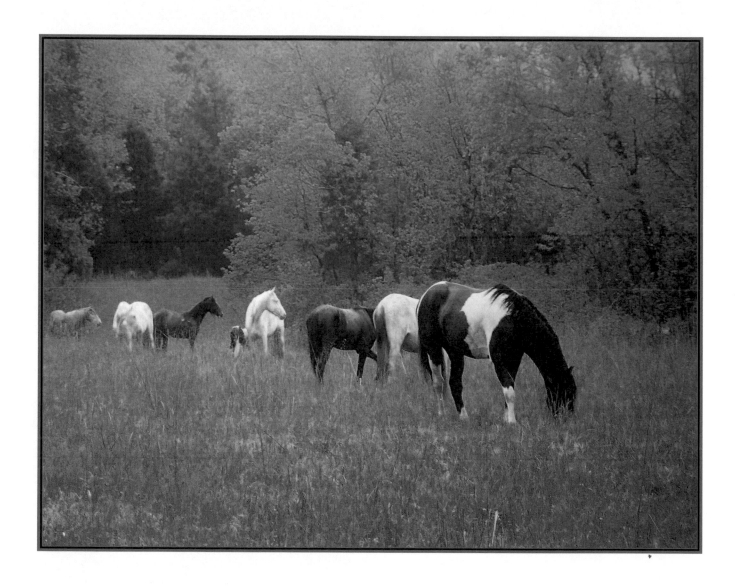

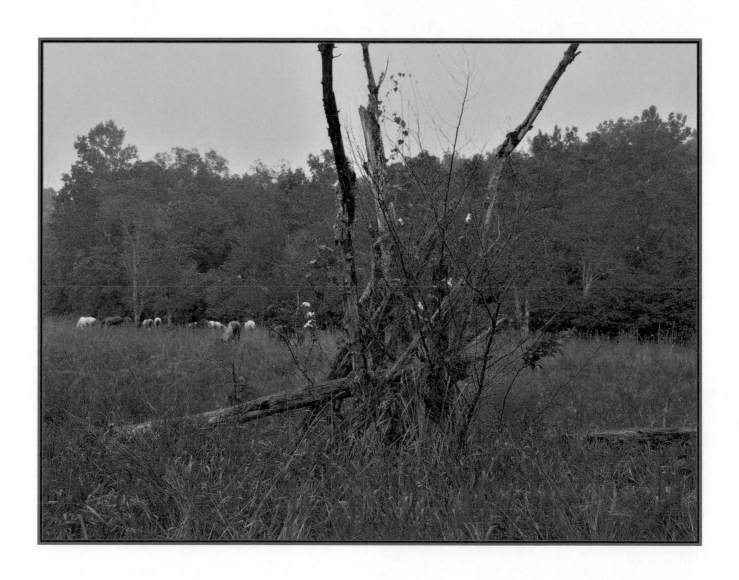

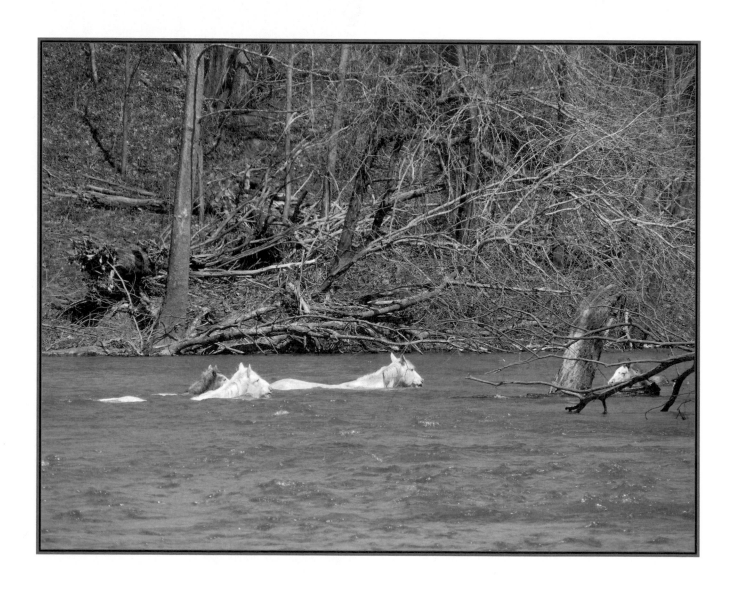

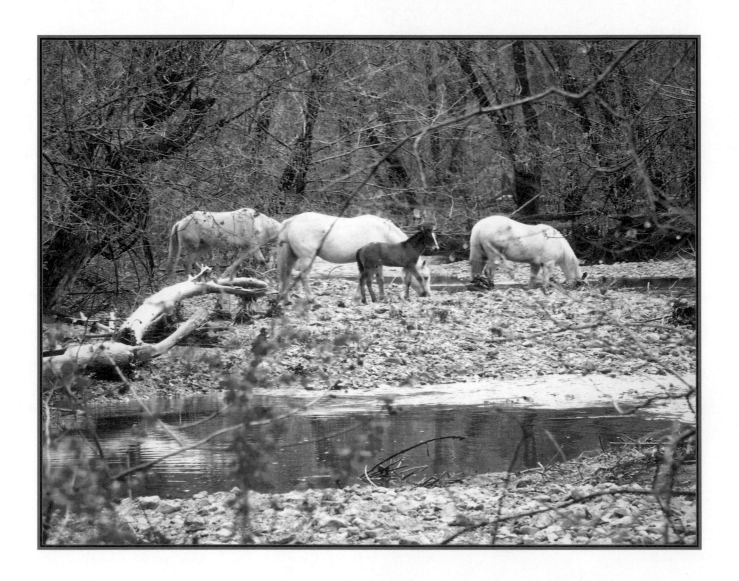

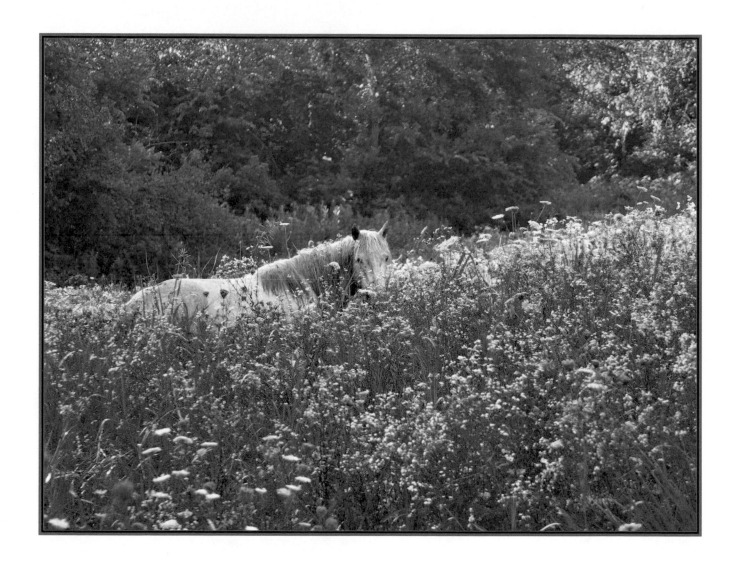

Printed in the United States
by Baker & Taylor Publisher Services